ACROSS GREEN PASTURES

Inspirational words for all time

BAYO FADUGBA

ACROSS GREEN PASTURES

Inspirational words for all time

GODKULTURE BOOKS

Across Green Pastures
by Bayo Fadugba
Copyright © 2014 All Rights Reserved

Paperback ISBN 978-0-9904637-0-2
e Book ISBN 978-0-9904637-1-9

Published by
GodKulture Books
Chicago, IL
Phone: 815 630 9890

Email:books@Godkulture.org

Cover Design: Baseline Concepts © 2014
Author Photo: Picture People © 2012

Printed in the United States of America

CONTENT

DEDICATION

To the sweet memory of my late parents:

Chief Akinbode Olumuyiwa Mosunmola Fadugba

(1920 – 2013)

Deaconess Margaret Olufunke Fadugba

(1941 – 2014)

ACKNOWLEDGEMENT

For an aspiration turned reality, all thanks and praise to God!

Big thanks to Sinmisola Ogúnyinka, my sister-in-law, who flamed the fire about getting the book done, and was resilient in her pursuit of it, and did extensive work on editing the raw scripts.

Tolu Oyeniran, who worked tirelessly to ensure the scripts were ready and properly presented at the right time - thank you so much.

I wish to thank every minister, staff and member of RCCG Dominion Chapel, Stafford, Texas for their love and contributions over the years to my life and ministry. Without you, the sermons collated in this book might never have been preached!

For your continual spiritual guidance and excellent leadership, Pastor James Fadele, I am grateful.

For the opportunity and privilege to be your son, Daddy (Pastor E. A. Adeboye), I will forever be thankful to God.

To my beautiful wife and #1 cheerleader who has always encouraged, inspired and supported me – Toun, I appreciate you and will always cherish you. You and our sons, Timi, Tomi and Tolu, create the right atmosphere in my life to thrive, to achieve and to succeed. Thank you. You all are the best!

INTRODUCTION

... it's part of God's plan for you to be a success...

Jeremiah 29:11 (NIV) says, "For I know the plans I have for you, declares the LORD, plans to prosper you and not to harm you, plans to give you hope and a future."

ACROSS GREEN PASTURES is a book of many messages packaged to set you on the course of destiny. God's plans are for our good, to take us to the expected destiny. All you need to do is set yourself in line with the word of God, and let God do the rest.

Everybody has a future, and a season to manifest in the hope for that future. Five things I have found useful to me as a person in focusing on the path God has chosen for me in fulfilling destiny are:

Set a goal: It is crucial to set a goal for every season. To set your goal, you need to first recognize the season. Life is in seasons (Ecclesiastes 3:1-9.) Set a goal for the season. Goals are the fuel in the furnace of achievement. It is important you know you should never plan God out of your goals for without God you will be disappointed.

Write down your goal: The only way to keep your vision in view is to write it down. Writing helps you to remember. When the vision is written, it can be shared with those who will help bring it to fulfillment.

Habakkuk 2:2 says, "Write the vision and make it plain on tablets, that he may run who reads it."

Have a plan, count the cost: Almost everything we achieve in life has a process and a cost. Research your vision, sit down and plan, and count the cost.

Write down the plan: This will also help to account for your progress, and adjust whenever there is need.

Start working the plan: Most importantly, make a move in the direction of your goal. Diligent Smart Work (DSW) under the covenant leads to sweatless success. Proverbs 21:25 says, "Despite their desires, the lazy will come to ruin, for their hands refuse to work." (NLT), and Proverbs 28:19 admonishes, "Work your garden—you'll end up with plenty of food; play and party—you'll end up with an empty plate." (Message Bible.)

BOOK 1
FAITH FOR GREEN PASTURES

The Product Power of Vision

The Season of Exodus

Excellence

Laws of Progress

CHAPTER 1
THE PRODUCT POWER OF VISION

…Sight is a function of the eyes. Vision is a function of the heart…

To have sight without vision is worse than being born blind. What are you living for?

A story is often told of two men bedridden in the same hospital room. One was bitter and unhappy. The other had a cheerful disposition toward life and his surrounding environment. He looked forward to getting healed and had a vision of his days after the being discharged, while his roommate lamented and cursed. Though both were physically blind, the cheerful one recovered faster than the bitter one. Why do you think this happened?

Vision is the capacity to see beyond your eyes. Eyes are meant to look. Vision is meant to see. Sight is a function of the eyes. Vision is a function of the heart. Vision means beginning a thing with the end in mind.

Genesis 1 says, "In the beginning, God…" God was before the beginning, but He did not leave the world in chaos. He conceived a dream and a vision of the world with the people in it. Then He began to create what He envisioned. At the end, God compared what He envisioned to what He created and saw that it was good.

From this point of view, I make bold to conclude that:

- ✓ You are not an accident.
- ✓ You are not a failure.
- ✓ You are a product of God's vision.

Psalms 139:13-16 explicitly shows that you are not a mistaken creature. Even when we hear of children conceived by 'mistake.' The mistake may be from your parents but never from God. Jeremiah spoke of God knowing him, and calling him even before he was born.

If you take a study of the conception process, you will realize that a race was won by you in order for you to be born. Many seeds ran toward the mark of the egg, but you got there and were conceived.

It leads to the realization also that anything done without prior vision will not yield any product.

Just like the story of the two blind men in the hospital room, your physical eyes may not get you where you want to be but your vision-eyes will.

Begin with a vision of where you want to be in the next week, and month, and year and eventually, when you are laid to rest, where you want people to remember you for being.

CHAPTER 2
THE SEASON OF EXODUS

… Exodus brings you to a new dawn…

In Exodus 5:9-13, we see a dreary situation God's people faced in the hands of their Egyptian masters.

It goes to show there is a period of darkness, which precedes the breaking of the dawn. There is a bursting forth of delayed blessings when you're propelled from obscurity to prosperity just as in the case of Moses who had been in the backside of life, tending sheep. He had some issues with who he was when God called him to lead the people of Israel out of the bondage of Pharaoh. Before he went though Moses asked God three questions:

1. Who am I? Moses wondered what special thing he had done that God would consider him able to accomplish such a task. He also asked God what should be said when he is asked, "Who sent you?"

2. What if they don't listen? Moses always considered himself to be a bad speaker.

3. Why can't someone else be sent? Moses considered that there were many others who could do a much better job than he could.

From the earlier scripture, you can just imagine the difficulty the Israelites faced, having to make bricks without a major material needed, and still without reducing productivity.

This happens a lot. Just at the time you expect that break, ugly situations crop up.

When Moses did succeed in bringing the nation of Israel out of Egypt, the enemy responded. The enemy pursued with drawn swords to utterly destroy the Israelites. But in attempting to do such an act, God responded and the earth swallowed them.

The season of Exodus is when you come out of bondage from the oppression of the enemy. It brings you to a new dawn. Exercise your faith, build it, and wait for your much-anticipated success. Enter your Exodus season with purpose.

CHAPTER 3
EXCELLENCE

… start with what you have and where you are …

What is excellence? Is it to be outstanding? To be exceptional? To be better?

God is an excellent God. His creation is excellent. Heaven is an excellent place. The human body reveals an excellent workmanship of a master craftsman.

Excellence must start with what you have and where you are. Moses started with just a rod. Daniel was located in a foreign land when God found him. Striving for excellence simply means making every effort in preparation and execution of everything you do in the service and worship of God.

What is mediocrity? Is it to be middle quality? To not be good enough? Mediocrity makes God unhappy (Revelations 3:15-16). Service to God less than excellent is not acceptable. (Malachi 1:6-8.)

There is always a "good reason" to offer God less than your best. Do you have a good reason to give God your leftover time, leftover money, and leftover energy? Are you giving God substandard service, unacceptable worship just because everyone else is doing it? The level of service we give to God reveals our attitude toward Him.

Service is meant to be costly.

God has already given us what we need to walk in excellence, but most of us keep looking out for external factors to change what's within. Outside forces do not control our character. We do! What you have and where you are and what you can do now is the greatest influence you have over your future. True greatness consists of being great even in the little things.

God is an excellent God and He expects us to walk in excellence in all spheres of our lives. Start from where you are, what you have, and what you can do right now. You will be amazed at how much potential you have inside of you! A few lessons from a sermon by Michael Luke:

1. There is always a reason to offer God less than your best. If you decide to, you will always find an excuse.

2. Service is meant to be costly. Time, money, energy are spent on service.

3. God expects and deserves nothing less than your best! There's no doubt about that. God keeps you alive and doing what you do.

So if you are not at the excellence point yet, you need transformation.

Why do we need transformation?

God demands it. We are all born into the corrupt Adamic nature (Romans 5:12-14.) Because of this we are all in need of salvation through the sacrifice Jesus Christ made at the cross (Colossians 1:12-14.)

At natural birth, you receive some benefits without being aware of them. You are given a family name. With this family name comes privileges and an inheritance such as wealth, love, skin color, etc. Well, a similar thing happens when you have a spiritual birth. Some benefits come with salvation. You are given a new name in Christ. You are given new privileges in Christ. You are shown the love, wealth and guidance found in the family of Christ.

There are other benefits as well. You are given divine inheritance, God's protection, and most importantly, you are given eternal life.

The proof of salvation is seen in some areas:

- You no longer sin willfully

- You are no longer full of lust

- Your attitude to the things of God is transformed.

Suppose a young man, Bob, comes back home from school and his father tells him to take out the garbage and wash the car. Those are specific commandments from his father and he obeys. But suppose Bob overhears his father say he wishes someone would mow the lawn and rake the leaves. Bob does it, not because he was asked to, but because he loves his father and wants to do not only his commandments, but also his word.

Our walk and talk ought to coincide. Our lives ought to be consistent with the way we talk. Think about the walk of Jesus. In His childhood He walked in submission to His parents.

In His earthly ministry He walked the dust roads of Galilee

healing, preaching, and doing good deeds to all people.

Transformation requires salvation, which requires identification with Christ in the daily Christian walk.

God also demands growth (Colossians 1:9-10), which is a function of transformation. You cannot transform if you don't grow. When you stop growing, you begin to die.

CHAPTER 4
LAWS OF PROGRESS

…Obey the principles of God for progress and you will increase…

It is part of God's plan for all to make progress (Jeremiah 29:11.)

He makes successful without adding tears and sorrow. Just as the lion and the bird are programmed to hunt and to fly, so also you have been programmed to succeed in life. He has come to stretch you to reach out for something more than you have right now. Until you stretch you cannot reach beyond what you have.

God is not a respecter of persons but a respecter of principles. Obey the principles of God for progress and you will increase your capacity for success. With the following principles adhered to, you can have a 50% assurance that you are on the right course.

1. Set a Goal for every season of life. (Ecclesiastes 3:1-9)

a. Recognize the season. As real as there is a time to be born and a time to die, so also a time to sow and a time to reap. Indeed there is a season, time, and purpose for everything.

b. Set the goal for this season. Goals are the fuel in the furnace of achievement. If you are aiming at nothing in life, you will ultimately hit nothing. A man with no destination will arrive at no destination. Where you land in 5, 10, or 20 years isn't by accident. It's a direct result of the goals you set TODAY.

c. Never plan God out of your goals. (James 4:13-15) It is good to have goals, but goals will disappoint us if we leave God out of them. There is no point in making plans as though God did not exist, because the future is in His hands. How will you react if God steps in and rearranges your plans? There is a possibility that God may readjust your plans to fulfill His will in your life. Will you still go for it? My dream was to become a successful lawyer, but God had another purpose for my life as a pastor. If I had refused I would have missed my mark in life.

2. Write down your goal for this season. (Habakkuk 2:2) Talk to God about this season now.

a. Have a plan. After you have written your goal and talked to God about it, you need to put a plan in place. Every goal needs to go through process to be achieved (Luke 14:28-30.) Embarking on a project without counting the cost often leads to a premature end. If you need to reach a certain level in your career, relationship, or spiritual walk, you need to have a plan on how to get there.

b. Make a move in the direction of your goal. Take the first step and you will be surprised God will move ahead of you (2 Kings 7:3-20.) Diligent smart work under the covenant leads to sweatless success.

c. Focus on the goal (Philippians 3:13b). FOCUS means Follow One Course Until Successful. Obstacles are those frightful things you see when you take your eyes off your goals. Les Brown says, "The one you focus on the longest, becomes the strongest."

d. Make up your mind. Your attitude determines your altitude. Great examples in scriptures are David and Goliath (1 Samuel 17:42-58), and Joshua and Caleb with the 10 Spies (Numbers 13:30-33.) The key to your success is in you. Stop blaming others for your own failures.

e. The season to succeed is NOW. Martin Luther King Jr. stated in his 1967 speech:

"We are now faced with the fact, my friend that tomorrow is today. We are confronted with the fierce urgency of now. In this unfolding conundrum of life and history, there is such a thing as being too late. Procrastination is still the thief of time. Life often leaves us standing bare, naked, and dejected with a lost opportunity . . ."

When you choose to work toward your goal, you choose to become what you set out to do. You then add value to yourself. From the beginning there were resources on the earth but they were not manifested until someone was ready to cultivate and use those resources.

I never knew that I could be a pastor until someone told me to lead a church. There are resources locked within you that unlock only when you begin to work.

BOOK 2
FAVOR FOR GREEN PASTURES

The Covenant of Financial Prosperity/Transformation

The Marriage that Works

Lessons for the unmarried, married and parents

CHAPTER 5
THE COVENANT OF FINANCIAL PROSPERITY/ TRANSFORMATION

…God expects us to produce results under the covenant…

Thoughts to keep in mind before we continue:

1. Admit that there are things you do not know.

2. Be willing to learn new things from the Lord who knows it all and has it all.

3. Personally apply the principles that God has used to raise others to financial prosperity.

4. Prepare to enjoy your wealth!

A brief study of the richest men on earth brought me to a shocking conclusion, which I desire to share. I discovered that the top 10 richest people in the world in the year 2010 are all investors! And I dare say it was not totally dependent on their worship of God, but rather obedience to principles of wealth.

No. 1   Carlos Slim Helu

Worth: $53.5 billion

Religion: Catholic

Investment: Invested heavily in telecom business in Mexico in 1990.

No. 2   Bill Gates

Worth: $53 billion

Religion: Not known

Investment: More than 60% of his investment is outside Microsoft; investments include Four Seasons hotels, Televisa, Auto Nation.

No. 3   Warren Buffett

Worth: $47 billion - Investments.

Religion: Agnostic

Known as America's favorite investor, he invested up to $10 billion in 12 months on surging Berkshire Hathaway shares, and shrewdly invested $5 billion in Goldman Sachs and $3 billion in General Electric amid the 2008 market collapse. Recently, he acquired railroad giant Burlington Northern Santa Fe for $26 billion.

These billionaires are all good investors of time!

Deuteronomy 8:18 says, "And you shall remember the Lord your God, for it is He who gives you power to get wealth, that He may establish His covenant which He swore to your fathers, as it is this day." This is a Biblical principle of wealth for believers, which when followed, we will experience tremendous breakthrough.

Each of us has a bank called time. Every morning, this bank credits us with 86,400 seconds, and every night it writes off as lost whatever of this not invested to good purpose. It carries over no balance. It allows no overdraft. Each day it opens a new account for you. Each night it burns the remains of the day.

If no deposits are made during the day, the loss is yours. There is no going back. There is no 'drawing against tomorrow'. You must live in the present on today's deposits. Invest it so as to get from it the utmost in health, happiness, and success! The clock is running. Make the most of today.

Benjamin Franklin said, "Do not squander time, for it is the stuff life is made of."

Let us use the four letters in the word TIME to help us learn its importance.

T - TREASURE

God expects us to treasure time as a valuable commodity. We number our years (or at least some of us do), but every day is precious and so we should treasure and number it.

- To realize the value of ONE YEAR, ask a student who failed a grade.

- To realize the value of ONE MONTH, ask a mother who gave birth to a premature baby.

- How valuable is ONE HOUR? Ask the businessman whose flight was delayed an hour and he missed an important business deal.

- How valuable is ONE MINUTE? Ask the man who had a heart attack in the restaurant and an EMT happened to be sitting at the next table and CPR saved his life.

- How valuable is A SECOND? Ask the driver who barely missed a head-on collision with an oncoming car.

- How valuable is A MILLISECOND? Ask the Olympic swimmer who missed qualifying by six-tenths.

Time really is valuable.

Learn these few things about what time means for you and your family, and treasure every moment that you have.

- Yesterday is history. Tomorrow is a mystery. Today is a gift. That's why it's called the "present."

- You can make more money but you cannot make more time.

- Have you ever heard the expression, "time is money?" But do you know time is much more valuable than money? It may be hard to make more money, but it can be done. But it is totally impossible to make more time.

- TIME is not only money; it is much more valuable than money.

A.W. Tozer wrote:

"Time is a resource that is non-renewable and non-transferable. You cannot store it, slow it up, hold it up, divide it up or give it up. You can't hoard it up or save it for a rainy day—when it's lost it's unrecoverable. When you kill time, remember that it has no resurrection."

So, we must understand the need to treasure time as the most valuable asset you are given in this world.

One common denominator amongst great men is that they are all time-conscious.

People usually see great achievements. What most do not see is the time it took to achieve them. Nothing great is achieved overnight. Great achievers have this in common: they recognize their mission will take time and with time comes adversity, failures and struggles.

They do know that with perseverance and consistent action, they will prevail and they do.

I - INVEST

Many of the phrases used about time are not really possible. For instance, we say, "I need to buy more time." Or, "I will make time…" In reality, these are just idioms. You can't buy more time and you can't really find or make more time.

You cannot even save time. If you do not use it, you lose it forever. In the early 1970s Jim Croce wrote a song that said, "If I could save time in a bottle, the first thing that I'd like to do, is to save every day till eternity passes away— just to spend them with you." Those are great lyrics, and it would be nice if we could save time, but you can't. In fact, a few months after he wrote that song, he was tragically killed in a plane crash in Natchitoches, Louisiana at the age of 30. You can't save time.

We have all kinds of "time-saving" appliances like the microwave oven. Guys love to take shortcuts in order to "save time." Show me some of the time you have saved—where is it? You cannot save it. You can only spend it on the choices you make.

However, you can invest time.

At the graduation commencement at his alma mater, Wheaton College, Billy Graham said, "Time is the capital that God has given us to invest. People are the stocks in which we are to invest our time, whether they're blue chips or penny stocks or even junk bonds."

Where you invest your time reveals what is most important to you. There are 168 golden hours in each week. The average person will spend about 56 of those hours sleeping, about 24 hours eating and for personal hygiene, and about 50 of those hours working or traveling to work. This means there are only about 35 hours a week of "discretionary" time left over. That's about 5 hours per day. Where do you invest those hours?

If I were to follow you around and observe you for those 5 hours, after about 10 days, I could tell you what is most important in your life. You might not like it, or agree with it, but for some of you, surfing the internet is most important to you. For others, watching television, or reading magazines is what's most important.

How much of that discretionary time are you devoting to your Lord? How much are you devoting to your family? A study of 1,500 households at the University of Michigan found mothers working outside the home spend an average of 11 minutes a day on weekdays, and 30 minutes a day on weekends with the children (not including mealtime.) Fathers spend an average of 8 minutes a day on weekdays and 14 minutes a day on weekends in different activities with their children.

* Time is life's greatest currency on earth. What you are today is the product of your time invested yesterday.

Life is in stages:

- Young age — morning time (1-30 years)

- Middle age - noon time (30- 50)

- Old age - evening time (50 and above)

Ecclesiastes 3:1-2a says, "To everything there is a season, and a time to every purpose under the heaven: a time to be born, and a time to die."

When you do not go to school when others are going to school you cannot graduate when others are graduating.

You do not have all the time. But you have enough.

Don't ever say you do not have enough time because you have exactly the same number of hours per day as was given to Michael Angelo, Mother Teresa, Leonardo DaVinci, Thomas Jefferson and Albert Einstein. How you spend your time shows the value you place on your life.

Proverbs 22:2 says, "The rich and the poor have this in common: The LORD made them both."

Time is the primary currency you exchange for everything in life. How you value your time determines the power of your currency.

Les Brown studies voraciously and corporations pay him $10,000.00 per hour to motivate their staff. People who earn high wages per hour invest time in acquiring the knowledge they use on the job.

M - MANAGE

All the money we receive comes from God and we only manage it. The same can be true of time. God is the creator of time, and He alone controls it.

A time management expert who taught at a seminar for executives placed a large, clear open-mouthed jar in front of the group. Next, he put seven or eight large rocks into the jar until it was full.

"Is the jar full?" he asked. Everyone nodded.

Then he took pebbles and filled up the jar with the small rocks until they reached the rim.

"Is the jar full?"

By now, they did not answer. He poured fine sand in.

"Is the jar full?" Some nodded.

He proceeded to take a pitcher of water and filled up the jar again.

"What's the lesson about time management?" he asked.

Hands shot up, and everyone agreed. "No matter how busy you are, you can always fit more things into your schedule."

"Wrong," he said. "The lesson is - unless you put the big rocks in first, they will never fit in. You must figure out what the big rocks are for you."

What are the big rocks in your life? Giving time to God? Giving time to your marriage and to your children? If you do not put those big rocks in first, someone else will fill up your jar. Understand this:

Every moment is a gift from God that must be managed wisely.

There is an entire field of study called "time management." In almost every business in America, consultants are hired to teach busy executives how to better manage their time. Time management is a hot topic.

In his book, Seven Habits of Highly Effective People, Stephen Covey writes, "Time management is a misleading concept. You can't really manage time. You can't delay it, speed it up, save it or lose it. No matter what you do time keeps moving forward at the same rate. The challenge is not to manage time, but to manage ourselves."

The Bible uses another word. Instead of managing your time, it speaks of "redeeming" the time," which is an even better idea. Paul writes Ephesians 5:15-16, "See then that you walk circumspectly, not as fools, but as wise, redeeming the time because the days are evil."

The phrase "walk circumspectly," means to be constantly looking around to make the most of every opportunity.

Emmett Smith was a great football running back, but he was not the biggest or the fastest, or the strongest. What he excelled at was running with his eyes open, and he was one of the best at seeing holes as they opened and then running through them. That is the way we should live, looking for every opportunity to invest time wisely, and then darting through them.

When an opportunity passes, it cannot be reclaimed, it is gone forever. That's what it means to redeem the time.

If you do not manage your time, someone else will manage it for you. You cannot save time, or even waste time—you are going to spend it somewhere and invest it in someone. If you do not control your schedule, someone will always be happy to do it for you.

Some people complain they just do not have enough time to spend with their family. You've got exactly the same amount of time as everyone else; you just aren't managing your time wisely or managing yourself wisely.

Suggestions on ways to manage time better:

- **Set daily goals** - you cannot develop a value of time until you learn to set goals. You cannot change your life until you change your time.

- **Identify time wasters** - including people!

- **Protect your time** - educate people around you to protect your time.

- **Keep moving**, even during slow periods.

- **An idle hand is the devil's workshop** – see David's example in 2 Samuel 11:1-3 "It happened in the spring of the year, at the time when kings go out to battle... But David remained at Jerusalem. Then it happened one evening that David arose from his bed and walked on the roof of the king's house. And from the roof he saw a woman bathing, and the woman was very beautiful to behold. So David sent and inquired about the woman..."

E - ENJOY

My focus will be on the time you spend with your family. This time should be enjoyed and not endured. It should be the best time of your life.

Nobody on their deathbed ever said, "I wish I had spent more time at work."

Several years ago, Ken Griffey, Jr. was invited to the "Players' Choice Awards" where he was to be awarded the player of the decade award. That's a big deal on national television. He beat out players like Barry Bonds and Mark McGwire. But when he found out when the award was to be given, he declined to attend. He had something more important to do. His five-year old son, Trey, was playing in his first baseball game.

One suggestion I have on how to enjoy the time of your life is learn to say NO to family-time robbers. There will always be something else to do and somewhere else to be, but if time with your family will be a priority, you have to learn the power of that two-letter word.

You need to understand that when you say, "YES" to family time, then you have already said, "NO" to everything else. But many parents allow interruptions and other demands distract them from the family time.

Fifty years from now, when you are old, aged and retired from active service, what will be more important—time with your family, or some television show?

T – Treasure

I – Invest

M – Manage

E – Enjoy

CHAPTER 6
THE MARRIAGE THAT WORKS

...Marriage is a covenant, and for every covenant, there are consequences...

I will put in a chapter for marriage here, not for necessity sake but by compulsion. Many marriages have been faced with untold distress.

To lie in green pastures, marriage must be for mutual fellowship. Dr. Otabil made a statement that he is closest to his wife more than any other person on the earth. He speaks with her more than any other person, and that is what the relationship in marriage should be like.

Marriage started in God. It was a God idea. It was God who said it is not good for man to be alone. Adam was not thinking about a wife. God found a wife for him, and conducted the first marriage. And if it started with God, it started in the spirit. Why then start something in the spirit, but try to accomplish it in the flesh?

We have been hoodwinked to believe that what we started in the spirit we can accomplish and finish in the flesh. It is important for all of us to see marriage from a spiritual prism. It is not just boy meets girl, get married and live ever after. If that is all marriage means to us, then we have lost the spiritual picture and God's agenda for marriage.

If we can only see that there is spiritual dimension to marriage, then we will understand the enormity and the responsibility of the assignment in marriage and we will not toy with it.

It is more than just wanting a tall dark and handsome man, or a slim, fair-skinned beauty queen. It's more than desiring the richest man, or a working lady who will not be a financial liability. Those things in themselves are not bad, but if that is all that marriage is, then it means marriage is in the flesh.

Flesh will tell you to look for all these things and these things alone, and flesh cannot discover the spiritual. Only the spirit can discern the spiritual.

As you depend on God for success in your spiritual walk, so should you also depend on God for your marital walk or desires. There is a God dimension to marriage, and until we see marriage from that perspective, we cannot capture the total spiritual essence of marriage.

The journey of life, for as much as we all see it, is a divine mandate on our lives, and before we leave this earth, destiny should be fulfilled. As we believe God for that, so also should we believe God that the total concept of marriage is not just about being beautiful, tall or slim. It is about God. The spiritual first, then every other thing will fall in place.

So when God tells you the educated to marry an uneducated gateman, because God said, and you do it, the end point is much greater than the beginning. The Bible says we serve God in the spirit, and have no confidence in the flesh. Everything about us is spiritual service and we put no confidence in the flesh.

To the covenant of marriage, some things we do, or do

not, may have long term effects not just on us, but on our children. The Godly choices we make preserve our heritage through several generations.

In life you may be able to bring water out of a rock (Num. 20:1-13), but yet there is a dark side to your life. When there is a consistent disobedience, never mistake the water coming out of the rock as divine approval for your misbehavior in life and in your marriage.

God said something profound when He rebuked Moses.

"Because I am a holy God, and you failed to show my holy nature to these people, your destiny is cut short (Num. 20:12.)"

The essence of God is holiness. It cuts deeper than words. It separates from darkness. Men may go through life and never touch that essence. I believe God wants to bring us back to the essence of His being.

The lesson to you is that when you fail to be teachable to the Spirit of God or the authority set in place by the Spirit of God, God will raise a donkey, an unusual situation to teach you (Numbers 22:1-41.)

My wife goes on business trips. And they tell her that after the business hours they would meet at a club, because most often they are men. It is important to take a stand for God at these moments. Some may have secret sin unpleasing to God or ungodly relationships. A few may have broken the covenant of marriage. You will need healing. You will need to cut off from such relationships no matter how difficult.

Loneliness is a façade and such human excuses are not spiritually acceptable to God. Come back home in your marriage, to the husband you may have despised, or that wife you may have trampled on.

The rule of thumb is to learn to play together, and learn to make fun with each other. Don't be too critical of each other. It is important you remain yourself in the relationship.

Marriage is to check the sinful life of adultery. A woman who refuses to come to church because she constantly tries to stay with her husband and make sure he doesn't commit adultery is not in a healthy marriage. Marriage is not just an agreement to live together till death do you part. It is a covenant, and for every covenant, there are consequences.

It has been statistically researched that 53% of marriages in America end in divorce. Amongst these statistics, marriage counselors were rated the most frequent in divorce. 36% of men and women admit to infidelity while on business trip. Once an affair has been discovered, only 31% of marriages last. Even higher, 74% of men and 68% of women admitted they would have an affair if they knew they would never get caught! These are staggering statistics to show marriage is under attack.

Marriage is ordained for the purpose of procreating and having children who fear the Lord and are raised according to His purpose. Sex within the confines of marriage is heavenly. When in doubt about a sexual act or style in marriage, don't do it.

Reconcile with God, for there is grace. Between you and your God.

CHAPTER 7
LESSONS FOR THE UNMARRIED, MARRIED AND PARENTS

…one of the things that sustain a home is the fear of God…

Genesis 49: 1-4.

"And Jacob called his sons and said, "Gather together, that I may tell you what shall befall you in the last days: Gather together and hear, you sons of Jacob, And listen to Israel your father. Reuben, you are my firstborn, My might and the beginning of my strength, The excellency of dignity and the excellency of power. Unstable as water, you shall not excel, Because you went up to your father's bed; Then you defiled it—He went up to my couch.""

There are three lessons I want to share from the scripture with three groups. The three groups are: singles who will get married, those who are married now and those who are parents. Every one of us fall under one of these three categories.

First group of people are not yet married, but someday will or permit me to say, may. In the choice of a marriage partner, ask God to choose for you. This is because there is a spiritual dimension to life.

Someone once said, "You are not ruined in life... until you marry the wrong person."

The second point for singles is all that glitters is not gold. Do not dwell on the physical alone. It is good to marry someone everyone acknowledges as beautiful. But it is important for you to know not everything that glitters is gold.

In Genesis 49, the Bible tells us about a man called Rueben. The description given by his father painted the picture of a man whose looks was excellent. Everything about his looks and his presence was dignified. The Bible however says his father placed a curse of instability on him, and because of this he would not excel in life. May you not be written off as a man or a woman not going anywhere. Amen.

The greatest tragedy of life is to get married to a woman or a man that would destroy your destiny. Reuben had everything on the outside. He looked like everything a woman would want to marry. Yet, though he seemed to have it all together on the outside, he was empty on the inside.

Because there is a spiritual side to marriage, the third advice for singles is to seek God on the choice of who to marry. God showed me my wife even when I wasn't praying about marriage or about her.

Some singles are so carried away by the looks of a potential partner; they fail to hear from God on the matter. It is important that you see this as an assignment and take it seriously.

Second group of people are married. Three things I will advise you are thus:

Number one: Some people assume that what sustains a marriage is how much you know about sex. If sex keeps homes and marriages together, then prostitutes would have the best of marriages. I believe one of the things that sustain a home is the fear of God. Pray for the fear of God in your marriage. The fear of God will keep you in check when your husband or wife is not there.

Pray the fear of God into the heart of your partner. There was one such wife who prayed that while she is not with her husband, no matter how much he is tempted, his "member" will not "be of use." Now that sounds like a playful and ridiculous prayer, but it is a very potent prayer.

When a man fears God, though a woman stands before him naked, the fear of God will cause him to run away much like Joseph in Potiphar's house.

Number two: Understand and respect the structure and hierarchy of God in the home.

1 Corinthians 11:2-4, "Now I praise you, brethren, that you remember me in all things and keep the traditions just as I delivered them to you. But I want you to know that the head of every man is Christ, the head of woman is man, and the head of Christ is God. Every man praying or prophesying, having his head covered, dishonors his head."

This scripture describes the hierarchy God has placed for the home. Naturally, the children fall under the authority of their parents. The theory that you are civilized, and everyone at the table has one vote, creating a democracy in your family is a recipe for disaster. God respects order and releases His grace, power, and authority accordingly.

The reason why the woman has a head is for her to be accountable to man, and the reason why the man has a head is for him to be accountable to Christ and not be a tyrant in the home.

Third group of people are parents. Three things for parents:

Proverbs 22:6, "Teach children how they should live, and they will remember it all their life."

The first thing: Be a model of what you want in your children. The best method of transferring knowledge is to be the model children can emulate. Have you not seen that once in a while when you find yourself in a tight corner the first thing that comes to your mind is how did your mother or your father do it? How did they settle matters about sibling rivalry? How did your mom pacify the children when dad was in a bad mood, and vice versa?

Often times our parents never specifically told us to watch and see how they did things. The monster we produce in our children at times is a result of what we showed and taught them.

Be a model of what you want in your children.

I have a study in my house. Many times my children run around and make excessive noise, and it has crossed my mind on more than one occasion to get a blind. But each time the Holy Spirit nudges me not to. For when they see me kneeling down in my study to pray, they will know daddy kneels down to pray. And when they find themselves in a tight corner beyond what their certificate or experience can handle, that same image will flash back. Let your children know that you do not know it all, but you serve a God who knows it all.

Teach your child and when they grow up they will not depart from it.

One morning as I prayed in my study, my eldest son got ready to go to school. Later, on the way to drop him off, he said I should pray for him too. It dawned on me then that he not only saw me praying, it registered with him.

The second thing: In Genesis 49 the Bible says Jacob called all his children and told them the different paths they would take. For you as parents, it is important to learn to manage the differences in your children because their destinies are different. The characters are different. Never compare one child to another, and never look down on a child for any reason at all.

The third thing: As parents, learn to give your children good and Godly memories. Part of the things we use to teach our children are the memories they receive from the Godly things we do. Those memories will guide them, such as memories of when you rolled on the floor and played with them. I found out that in life, the things we remember about our parents are few. For the children's sakes, make them moments of good memories.

I have said before that the first calling of everyone is our home. It is so important for you to pray for your home. For singles, pray for God to show you the partner He has for you. For married couples, pray for the fear of God in your hearts and in your marriage. And for parents, pray that God would make you the right model.

Men, if your children see you slap your wife, you may not believe it but one day that child may grow up and begin to slap his wife as well, except God steps in. What stops me from ever raising my hand against my wife is Christ. I am sad to recall but I grew up seeing my dad beat my mom. But I made up my mind that the beating my wife "deserves" by my dad's standards had already been received by my mother. Because Christ came into my life, He gave me the grace to stand and never raise my hand against my wife.

Now I am talking about very serious issues.

If you do not know this God as your God, you will make bad choices like Reuben. You will choose a man or woman who comes to church but is unstable in his Christian walk. I urge you to make Jesus the Lord of your life, and trust Him to help you with important choices. Unstable waters could come in any form to destabilize your life and destiny. Build your home on the foundation that is Christ.

BOOK 3
HOPE FOR GREEN PASTURES

The House of Lydia

Protecting the Unity of the Church

Benefits of Unity

Where disunity thrives

CHAPTER 8
THE HOUSE OF LYDIA

...there is a place for you...

Mark 16:15-20.

God expects us to take the gospel of His kingdom to all parts of the earth. And as Jesus instructed them they went. They stepped out of their convenience; they stepped out of their comfort zones; they stepped out of their culture and they went. And the Bible says Jesus went with them. Signs and wonders attended to them.

If only we will obey and go.

Samuel said to King Saul it is better to obey than to offer the fattest sacrifices. For some of us we have reversed the scripture. We want to offer sacrifices of our service, of everything else rather than being an instrument of good news to this generation. To obey is much more important to God than the hefty sacrifices.

The sacrifices of thanksgiving will not be acceptable if it is brought on the platter of disobedience. God said, "Go into all the world and make disciples of all nations..."

Throughout last year how many disciples did you make? How many people did you preach to with your life? With your words? With your gifts? How many people did you expressly reveal the love of God so much to that they ask about your God and what they must do to be saved?

God said when we obey signs and wonders will attend to us. Healing will become the children's bread for us. Deliverance will come easy. When we obey everything else we trust God for will come to us. And the only thing God asks is that we take the baton.

The Bible says that every where Jesus went preaching the gospel of the kingdom, he taught by example. If you ask me how I know we have not been preaching the gospel of the kingdom of God I would tell you to look around you. Each empty chair in church represents a soul that you are meant to impact for the kingdom.

Remember the earthquake, consequence of Paul and Silas' praise. The jailer, an unbeliever asked what he must do to be saved? Now, please ask yourself, "When was the last time someone asked me what they must do to be saved?" When last did someone say, "You have touched my life. I have watched you in this office for so long. When they are talking about sin you don't as much as join them to laugh about filthy things. The way you carry yourself. Your life has been an inspiration to me. Can I know the God you serve? Why are you different?" Has anyone ever felt the impact of your prayer and worship?

The Bible says the disciples went with signs and wonders following. The beauty of our faith is not in carrying the biggest bibles, or living in large houses, or driving the nicest cars. It's not in just being blessed. The beauty of our faith is in the demonstration of the power of the kingdom of God and signs and wonders. It is in living without compromise. In your workplace, you will be a marked man or a marked woman because they will be watching you. Even if they are not living up to the Christian standard, they know what is expected of an average believer.

This is why many hide their identity at the place of work, or in the neighborhood. They know that if they associate us as being believers, yet our lifestyle does not correlate with what we profess, it brings about shame to the kingdom.

In the book of Acts 16, the Bible tells us about a unique story under the topic of missions, because missions do not necessarily have to be in Nicaragua, Panama, or El Savador. Mission work is not until we go out to India. In your own city, you can find enough mission fields. Mission work can happen in the neighborhood you live in. You can start a bible study, a fellowship, or start taking care of the children on the block. And while doing it let them know there is something different about you.

It is important for you to know that mission work can only be done under the leading of the Holy Spirit. You must first listen to what God is asking you to do, and when He instructs you please do not be disobedient to the Spirit of God.

Paul and Silas had dedicated their lives to serving God, and so decided to go to Asia because there was no church there. The Bible says however that the Holy Spirit forbade them from going. Even though it made intellectual sense for them to go to Asia, the Holy Spirit forbade them because the Holy Spirit had the plan.

The truth is the plan that would yield the maximum results is not the plan of man. The plan of man cannot do the work of the spirit in the power of the flesh. You cannot please God in the flesh.

The Bible says the same Holy Spirit who stopped them from going to Asia orchestrated events and stirred up a vision for Paul to go to Macedonia instead of Asia. So he went in the direction the Holy Spirit led him. But while he was on his way, he had to go through a certain city to pray. There he met a lady called Lydia.

Lydia was an ungodly business woman from Asia. And the Bible said Lydia accepted the gospel preached to her, and pleaded with them to come and visit her home. When they were following her to her home, they had to pass through a city called Phillippi. While in that city there was an encounter with a very powerful lord who had a child with a spirit of divination. This child could see into the future, yet recognized them as children of God.

Be careful who you allow to speak into your life. Some visions they see are right, but they come from a wrong spirit. You need to rebuke and reject it, because at times we get carried away by every powerful man that can "see" our future.

This child had the spirit of divination. Paul became irritated by the spirit and rebuked it. They took them to court and threw them in jail. While in jail, we know what happened: the singing, and praying, the earthquake, which led to the jailer's salvation. Yet the foundations of the jail were left intact. A targeted missile from heaven hit everything that needed to be hit from the first door to the inner door, including the chains. And yet the foundation was left untouched. The jailer gave his life to Christ, and the conclusion of the story was that Paul and Silas left the prison and entered into the house of Lydia. We should read this story from Acts 16.

When you make up your mind to obey God and become an

instrument, a witness for the gospel, there will be challenges. There will be opposition. In fact for some of us, the challenges we are facing right now have nothing to do with you, or some wrong you've done. It is simply because there is a mandate from Heaven over your life, and the enemy is all out to ensure that the destiny, the future, and the mandate do not speak in your time or in your generation.

The challenges some are facing with their children are just a distraction so they will not focus and do the work of the kingdom. Some while in the middle of service to God, get questioned on why they are serving God in the first place. Somebody you trust may come and question those following you, accusing you of trying to become a celebrity. In doing this, they discourage the structure God set in place to ensure the load the leader carries does not crumble on top of him or her. With their mouths they send satanic arrows, sometimes unknowingly. They question why you are following the leader so sheepishly, thus glorifying the enemy.

Remember, when Moses was mourning the death of his sister Miriam, the people were crying for water. Moses became so angry and upset that instead of speaking to the rock, he struck the rock and God became angry with him. This led to the greatest error of the ministry of Moses. You and I will not make an error that will destroy our destinies because of satanic voices speaking discouragement to the people of God in Jesus' name.

As a leader, I understand completely what Moses went through. But to go for God, you must be ready for such pain, discouragement, and attacks, even from the most trusted people around you. Until you pass the test of the prison, you may never get to the place God has prepared for you.

The Bible says Paul and Silas stepped out of the prison and entered into the house of Lydia. Lydia means "the place."

There is "the place" God has prepared for you and I, and the route to "the place" is not just walking a straight line. The route and the direction to "the place" may be through the prison. Until you pass the test of the attacks of the tongues of men, the discouragements… when you turn to either side and there are no friends. . . until you pass that test, you cannot get to "the place."

Men want to go to the palace without passing through the P.I.T (Prophet In Training.) If you are going to go you must obey and stay the course, even through the hardship that will come with it.

The place God has prepared for you and me is not through hard work alone. It requires the grace of God. What I have found out about the irony of life is that as difficult as it is, no destiny in God can be fulfilled alone. The plan of God for your life is bigger than your ability.

I want to leave everyone who reads this book with a conviction that there is a place for you. There is no need to compare yourself, your marriage, or your journey with someone else's.

There is "the place" and it is called the House of Lydia. There is a divine pattern and there is a season.

CHAPTER 9
PROTECTING THE UNITY OF THE CHURCH

…harmony and unity in a church can compare to the oil that drives a car…

Are you an instrument of unity?

From the book of Psalms, chapter 133, we see a self-explanatory scripture on the beauty and pleasantness of dwelling in unity. Harmony and unity in a church is comparable to the oil that drives a car. Compared to a man in need of Grace, or Anointing, God is saying seek after harmony. Ensure that in your heart, in your spirit, in your mind, you don't have anything against anybody.

Verse three of Psalms 133 talks of the refreshing dew as the place of harmony where God has commanded blessing. The place of unity in the home, as well as in the marriage, is where God has commanded blessing. The place of unity in the church is where God has commanded blessing, and when everyone comes to church, no one comes to church to be cursed, but rather to be blessed. For you to access that blessing you need to be in that place of unity.

When you reach that place of unity, it becomes difficult to harbor bitterness. Bitterness of heart hinders you from the presence of the Lord. It blocks access to the blessings of heaven.

This blessing is not of sleeping and waking, rainfall, and the sunshine on everyone, but the blessing that changes and transforms lives and destiny. One single meeting and an encounter with God can bring that blessing.

It is important for us to understand there are challenges, and it is just a matter of time before we step on each other's toes, but you cannot fulfill destiny and become what God wants you to be without people. The Bible says in Proverbs 14 and verse 4, without oxen, a stable stays clean. But you need strong oxen for large harvests.

I was in Ghana sometime ago and I saw a castle built during the time of slavery. It is unfortunate that the slavery we assume is over still takes place. This time however, the slavery is personal, and not physical but spiritual, and the slave masters are none other than strange spirits. When we give in to seducing spirits, spirits that divide, it opens the door wide and it is like you have sold the entire body. It's just like you have sold your neighbor, or a part of your body to the enemy. And of course the enemy takes advantage.

The visit to Ghana blew my mind. I saw prisons for male and female, and a door tagged "the door of no return." Through this door, the slaves left their homes forever. They either die on the ship or end up on one island or another. The guide locked us in a cell for a few minutes, and I believe I experienced hell. To imagine people here for weeks, and some left to see their fellow prisoner die and rot must be a terrible experience, to say the least.

What brings this Ghana experience to fore is the fact that we have kept prisoners of our brethren. We have a choice to pursue love and unity, overlook offense, and free brethren from the spirit of lock-down, and slavery knowing full well no human is perfect. We ourselves are not perfect.

No matter how much pain people cause us in a place of work, at home, or in church, forgive. Let go and let God take you to the next level. Without people in your life, it is near-impossible to fulfill destiny. No man has ever made it alone. Even Lone Ranger had a sidekick named Tonto. We need people, and at times we need the people who caused us pain.

In his final moments before his arrest, Jesus passionately prayed for unity. Christ knew the key to the growth and success of the church was unity, so he cried out to God for the Church to remain one. It is important we make every effort to keep the unity of the Spirit. Go the extra mile to protect it.

There is a story in the old times of a general who had four columns of soldiers, and wanted to take over a fortressed city. He had a plan he shared with his soldiers to calm their anxiety, to use his fifth column to take over the city. The soldiers reminded him there were only four columns. The general answered there were five. The fifth column was inside the fortress.

"When I get the signal, they would open the door from the inside. From there we will take the city," the general said confidently.

Quite a good number of us are fortresses, but we need to deal with the fifth column deep within threatening to open our doors from the inside. From there the enemy is able to infiltrate.

We need to build a culture free of class, race, and wealth. It is important for us to learn to treat people with respect and not look down on anyone, and not relate with each other based on class.

The Bible says if you favor some people above others, you are committing a sin, James 2:2-6. The circumstances of our birth, or ability to speak well matters least in God's agenda, for there is a God in heaven and he takes a man from the dunghill and puts him to sit with princes. There is a God and as he wills, he takes from the rear, and puts at the front. Your qualifications don't make you, but what you carry on the inside. God in you is the hope of glory.

To improve the quality of our relationships, we need to refrain from certain action, and usage of certain words, and be more cautious of the things we do. Statements like, "I am more qualified than the person they put ahead of me," is a divisive statement with a strong negative spiritual undertone. Be cautious of such statements and people who make them, for God sets people in the church, puts people in positions of leadership. Nothing happens without God's knowledge. Regardless of age, education, ability or otherwise, we still need to give them honor and respect.

In Matthew 25 verse 21, the Lord said, "well done my good and faithful servants." Gifting may make room but does not guarantee your position. Instead, your good hearts and motives do. How faithful and diligent are you with what God has committed into your hands? God did not welcome my gifted servant, but rather <u>my faithful servant</u>. You cannot be faithful to a God you cannot see, when you're not faithful to the people you can see.

The test of loyalty—our commitment and love to God and the bond of unity—in any situation and circumstance is measured in hard times. Will you continue to stand by the word of faith and testimony in the times of trials? Do you have an independent spirit in the church? So when a fast is called for Wednesday, you say your fast will be on Friday. Independent spirits lead to rebellion many times and can take you out of the camp.

In 2 Samuel 18:5-15, David the king, gave specific instructions, but his general decided to act independently, and in the process, some of the soldiers joined him in killing Absalom, David's son. The same general would later turn on King David.

Someone with an independent spirit becomes available for the enemy's use. If you're in the house be in the house. Let us have one vision. Let us have one direction. I hope we do not have independent spirits in our church! I have searched my heart, and I ask that you also search your heart. Do you have an independent spirit?

I mentioned this earlier and wish to emphasize on it. Offense can easily take root in the heart. Offense must come as a sign of the end time. If we are truly a family, offense must come. We all have weaknesses and faults. We step on one another's toes, but we must not let it take root. Offense opens the door to bitterness, and sometimes demonic infiltration, and it fights unity of the body.

CHAPTER 10
BENEFITS OF UNITY

…peace, love and unity create a pleasant atmosphere…

How do we gain from being united?

Going back to the text of the previous chapter, Psalms133, it's obvious unity breeds a peaceful and joyful atmosphere. Sometimes in the home front when a husband and wife are not in agreement, or between children and parents, though there is no outward exchange of words or angry outbursts, you can sense the tension. The opposite is true when there is peace, love and unity; the atmosphere is pleasant, filled with joy much more conducive for the power of the Holy Spirit to move.

Another gain of unity is that it provokes the blessing of God. In Psalms 133:3, we see God command His blessing, even life forevermore. There are people who do not enjoy the fullness of life and cannot access this blessing of God. They may need to find ways to forge unity, at work, school, home and church.

Unity creates a conducive atmosphere for the blessing. The key that unlocks the door is a heart that is right with God. There are some things God demand and expects from us. Unity is one of them.

To access the fullness of the blessing, we are required to walk in unity. The urge to speak what's on your mind may be great; to prove you could not be trampled on anymore. But the glory you're carrying is greater than your need to assert and affirm. Ask the Lord Almighty to restore back every glory lost due to ignorance, anger, misunderstanding, and the excess of our lips and our tongues. Amen.

The third benefit is that unity brings divine multiplication of power, strength, and achievements. I want us to do the math together. Deuteronomy 32:30. One will chase one thousand and two would put ten thousand to flight. This math is simple. Two united people will achieve ten times more than one person. Leviticus 26:8. Again let's do the math. The more united we are, the greater our results.

The table of the Lord is the most potent and powerful covenant. A fourth benefit comes when we are unified together at the Lord's Table. Strange and unimaginable things take place. Cancer can fall off. Things God did before can happen in our time and in our generation. Sicknesses can disappear because that token is much more powerful than any medication.

But the reverse is the case when we are divided. When there is a split. When somebody's not greeting the other. Whatever it is. The enemy knows at times we are coming for communion, so he sets us up. So on your way, the enemy reminds you of something, and you're totally disconnected by the time you step into God's presence. Then, you won't be a part of the blessing.

Unity makes the church a positive attraction to the world and this is my fifth benefit. There's nothing attractive about strife and division. Nothing draws the world to Christ when we are divided.

Nothing makes marriage beautiful when husband-and-wife is divided. Kids who grow up in homes where there is strife sometimes do not look forward to getting married.

So many other benefits apply.

Unity increases revelation. Unity builds trust. Prayer is effective when there is unity. It is a waste of time to pray when there is disunity because there's already a barrier blocking the prayer.

Unity brings out boldness and humility. The fact that you are able to do some things and not others does not make you superior or inferior to anyone. God wants unity, not necessarily uniformity. We need to be able to celebrate our differences. When you see a wife who talks much more than her husband, does not mean her husband is more spiritual or less independent. It is because God brings people with different strengths and weaknesses together.

A story about a customer and a tech-support comes to mind. The tech-support asked what can be done and after listening to the problem and much consideration decided to install love. The customer asked if he could be guided through the process. The tech-support said the first step is to open the system. The customer said that he had several programs running, like past hurts, low self-esteem, grudge and resentment, and asked if it was still okay to install love while these programs were on.

The tech-support said, "No problem, since love has the capacity to gradually erase harmful programs from your current operating system. It may remain in your permanent memory, but will no longer disrupt other programs. Love will eventually override all of these programs and install a module called high self-esteem.

However, you have to completely turn off grudge and resentment. Those programs prevent love from being properly installed. Can you check on those programs, and turn them off?"

The customer said, "I don't know how to turn them off."

Tech-support said, "Go to your start menu, and invoke forgiveness. Do this as many times as necessary until grudge and resentment are completely erased."

The customer said, "Love has started installing itself, is that normal?"

Tech-support said, "Yes but you have only the base program. You need to begin connecting to other hearts. This is in order to get the other upgrades."

The customer said, "I have an error message already. It said the love program is not meant to run on external hardware."

The tech-support said, "Love program is meant to be installed on internal systems only, but has not yet been run on yours. In short, you have to first love yourself before you can love others."

The customer asked, "What should I do then?"

Tech-support said, "Pull down self-acceptance, then click on the following file, forgive self, realize your worth, acknowledge your limitations. Now copy them to the "my heart" directory. The system will over write all conflict files. It will then begin patching faulty programs. Also you need to delete self-criticism from all directories and empty your recycle bin. This makes sure they are completely gone and never come back."

The customer said, "Got it! Hey, my heart is filling up with new files! Smile is playing on my monitor. Peace and contentment are copying themselves all over my hearts! Is this normal?"

Tech-support said, "Sometimes, but for others it may take a while. Eventually everything works at the proper time. So love is installed and running. One more thing before I hang up. Love is freeware. Be sure to give it and its various modules to everyone you meet. They will in turn share it with others. They will also return some cool modules back to you."

Customer said, "Thank you, God."

God is the tech-support. The customer is you and I.

Though we aspire for the ideal church where everything is perfect, what we have is the real church, because we are all humans, with different strengths and weaknesses. We ought to uphold those who fall, and lift them up. Let us build one another. If you keep looking for the perfect church, you will be disappointed.

CHAPTER 11
WHERE DISUNITY THRIVES

…disunity breeds strife and pain…

Just as we relish the benefits of unity, we must also be aware of the opposite of these benefits.

I could assume we know the import, and leave it out, but let's take a good look at it.

a. Where unity breeds peace and joy, (Psalm 133:1), disunity breeds strife and pain.

b. Where unity breeds the blessing, (Psalm 133:3), disunity brings curses.

c. Where unity breeds protection, Satan uses disunity to attack individuals. But when the church stands together, any attack toward one member is an attack at all members (1 Cor. 12:24-26.)

d. Where unity breeds multiplication of power and strength and thus multiplication of achievements as the Bible says one will chase one thousand, and two, ten thousand, and also in Lev. 26:8, five will chase a hundred and a hundred, ten thousand. Multiplication of achievement level five times! It then means strength depends on unity, and therefore, disunity weakens our strength and stunts multiplication or in essence facilitates division.

e. Where unity breeds the revelation of God's power to save and deliver souls, disunity fights the essence of Christ's message of salvation and prayer to God, "that they may be one as we are one," John 17:22.

f. Where unity breeds fulfillment and each member is working in his or her proper calling, and doing so, fulfilling the call of God individually and corporately, disunity brings strife.

g. Where unity breeds love, 1 John 4:20-21, disunity leads to desolation.

h. Unity attracts God's presence (Matt. 18:19-20), thus disunity attracts the devil's presence.

So whose presence do you carry about? Whose presence do you attract? Whose presence do you want?

BOOK 4
GRACE FOR GREEN PASTURES

I Call Him Lord

Prayers - Intimate Fellowship with God

Gifts of the Holy Spirit

That I may know Him

CHAPTER 12
I CALL HIM LORD

…Your faith is as strong as the adversity it survives…

God did not promise a Christian life without challenges and unexpected times of crisis.

At times the unexpected is the prelude to an expected visitation. When God was ready to promote Joseph, he arranged the entire country to experience famine and crisis.

Your faith is as strong as the adversity it survives! The wise man is the one who comes to Christ through salvation, hears His sayings and instructions, and does them through obedience. He is the one who builds his life on the principles of Christian discipleship as are laid down in the word of God. This is the right way to build a life.

Therefore according to Luke 6:46-49, when floods and streams batter the house, it stands firm because it is founded on the rock, on Christ and His teachings.

A poem states:
Ye call me the "Way" and walk me not,
Ye call me the "Life" and live me not,
Ye call me "Master" and obey me not,

If I condemn thee, blame me not.

Ye call me "Bread" and eat me not,
Ye call me "Truth" and believe me not,
Ye call me "Lord" and serve me not,
If I condemn thee, blame me not.

- Anonymous

Religious people are hearers but not doers. True Christians are doers and not just hearers. Religious people want God to do everything for them without their efforts. Religious people want immediate response from God and if He delays they stop believing in Him.

The word "Lord" means Master. It means that Christ has complete authority over our lives, and we belong to Him, and we are obligated to do whatever He says. To call Him Lord and then fail to obey Him is absurdly contradictory. True love and faith involves obedience.

You don't really love Him and don't really believe in Him if you don't really do what He says.

CHAPTER 13
PRAYERS - INTIMATE FELLOWSHIP WITH GOD

...Intimacy with God gives you access...

Genesis 3:8-9.

God is asking many of His children this same question, "Where are you?"

Prayer brings intimacy with God. Real intimacy starts on the outside and ends on the inside. Many people undermine the power of prayer, probably because of many new age teachings on the "how to." The do-it-yourself syndrome has given many the false impression that as long as they follow process and principle, the expected end will be met.

Remember that earlier in this book, I stated that your planning sure guarantees 50% of your success. The remaining 50% is the God-factor of which prayer is key.

I have seen people think they are intimate with God because they belong to a "prayer" Church or the "prayer department" in their churches. But prayer does not start at the prayer meeting but in the place of continual intimacy with God before and after prayer meeting, church meeting, etc.

Intimacy with God can be achieved in the prayer closet where you can be quiet and commune personally with God.

Intimacy with God gives you access to power to prevail in the circumstances of life and we know access to God makes it easy to resolve difficult matters (Isaiah 65:22-24.)

When you are intimate with God, dealing with gates become easy. As we know, gates represent establishments, barriers, opportunities and authority. We all face gates in our marriages, family life, career, social life and spiritually.

To deal with gates, you need to know:

- The size of the gate: This is determined by the treasure in the home within the walls.
- The nature of prisoners determines the gate, and the security posted there.
- A gate could be a hindrance on the journey to our promised land.

Remember Jericho and the children of Israel.

Intimacy with God provides the key to getting rid of gates!

CHAPTER 14
GIFTS OF THE HOLY SPIRIT

…Christianity is tedious without the help of the Holy Spirit…

Many people don't grasp the role of the Holy Spirit, and if the purpose of a thing is not known, abuse is inevitable.

Hence, many people struggle through life when they could have depended on the Holy Spirit, our helper. 1 Corinthians 12:7 says, "But the manifestation of the Spirit is given to every man for the profit of all."

Take note of these facts about the gifts of the Holy Spirit:

- Christianity is tedious without the help of the Holy Spirit.

- The gifts belong to the Holy Spirit and He is the only one who gives them.

- No man must take His glory neither should any man pay money for the gifts of the Holy Spirit (Acts 8:18-20.)

- The Holy Spirit gives them at His discretion, according to the measure of grace on your life (Romans 12:6, Ephesians 4:7.)

- The gifts are given for kingdom purposes and not for personal gain.

- It is through the gifts of the Spirit that we are able to minister effectively, to the world and to each other the comfort of the Holy Spirit (1 Corinthians 14:3,12)

- Salvation is a prerequisite to accessing the gifts of the Spirit.

The nine gifts of the Holy Spirit can be found in 1 Corinthians 12:4-11. These are categorized into three: Revelation gifts, Power gifts, and Vocal gifts.

The Revelation Gifts

1. Word of Wisdom

2. Word of Knowledge

3. Discerning of Spirits

Collectively, these three gifts are supernatural manifestations of the Spirit of God to give revelations.

The gift of word of wisdom is a supernatural perspective to ascertain the divine means for accomplishing God's will in a given situation, and is a divinely given power to appropriate spiritual intuition in problem solving. Furthermore, this gift involves having a sense of divine direction, being led by the Holy Spirit to act in a given set of circumstances, and rightly applying knowledge. The temptation of Jesus (Luke 4:1-14.)

The gift of word of wisdom is the application of knowledge that God gives you (1 Corinthians 2:6-7.) This type of wisdom is a gift which cannot be gained through study or experience, and it works interactively with the other two revelation gifts.

The word of knowledge is supernatural understanding of circumstances, situations, problems, or a body of facts by revelation, without assistance from any human resource but solely by divine aid (Elisha and Gehazi, 2 Kings 5:20-27.) Knowledge is raw material and wisdom builds upon it.

Discerning of spirits is the supernatural ability given by the Holy Spirit to perceive the source of a spiritual manifestation and determining whether it is of God (Acts 10:30-35), of the devil (Acts 16:16-18), of man (Acts 8:18-23), or of the world. It is not mind-reading or the ability to criticize or find fault. It implies the power of spiritual insight, it is a gift which protects and guards your Christian life. Other ways of discerning spirits include:

a. Observing what a person does (Matthew 7:15-20.)

b. Observing whether a person exalts Jesus Christ as the Son of God and as Lord and Savior (1 Corinthians 12:3.)

c. By listening to what a person says and seeing if it lines up with the truth of God's word (1 John 4:1-3.)

The Power Gifts

1. Gifts of Faith

2. Working of Miracles

3. Gifts of Healings

These three gifts will show forth God's glory, His power, His greatness, His majesty and His victory over sickness, disease and over death in supplying the needs of His people. The power gifts are for deliverance and overcoming nature itself.

The Vocal Gifts

1. Gift of Tongues

2. Interpretations of Tongues

3. Prophecy

Collectively, these three gifts are supernatural manifestations of the Spirit of God and through them God can speak through man what He chooses to make known either for the moment or the future.

CHAPTER 15
THAT I MAY KNOW HIM

… The pursuit of Christ will cost your time, your talent, and your treasure …

To know Him means to gain a practical day-to-day acquaintance with Him in such an intimate way you would become more Christ-like.

God wants the life of Christ to be reproduced in you. The pursuit of this life of Christ will cost your time, your talent, and your treasure. If you fail God in this area, He is able to find a substitute because no man can hold God to ransom and there is no vacuum in the realm of the spirit.

When Moses failed God in the wilderness of Zin, God raised Joshua to lead the people into the promise land. When Eli failed God, Samuel was raised to be the prophet. When Saul failed, David took his place (1 Samuel 16:1.) When Peter failed by refusing to be responsible for the Gentiles coming to know Christ, God raised Paul.

Let us be supernaturally propelled to pick up our lost destiny and fulfill it so that we will not fail God.

No one wants to be replaced. No one wants to fail. Even the people mentioned above never set out to be dropped. They all started well. Therefore, to be sure you will not fail God, you need to know Him, and serve Him. A life of service to God can only be total to be acceptable. Hence, bondservanthood.

So then, who is a bond servant?

1. A man of servile condition, a slave.

2. One who gives himself up to another's will whose will is used by Christ in extending and advancing His cause amongst men.

3. One who is devoted to another to the disregard of his own interests.

4. Someone who was purchased.

A concise acronym to help us live a life of such servitude to Christ is:

I.M.P.A.C.T – I Must Produce A Christ-Transformed life.

A life that must make impact will fight constant battle between light and darkness. Spiritual warfare is real, and there are spirits seeking to derail every child of God from taking actions for God (2 Timothy 2:3-5.) To make an impact for God, we must be ready for war!

To make impact we must also be ready to exercise divine authority over the powers of darkness no matter how fierce the situation. Light represents righteousness, holiness, joy, and every good thing God represents. Darkness represents every bad thing the devil represents—strife, sickness, weeping, affliction, bondage, disobedience, etc. Your prayer should always be for God to remove every trace of darkness in you, and grant you the grace to sustain the presence of the Holy Spirit, so you can alter or change a sinful pattern of life, style, thought or stronghold of one's mind.

This is sometimes seen in culture changes. Until you change the culture of a people, you cannot change them. We must provide an alternative to fun laced with sin. To make an impact through influence will require your time, your talent, and your treasure. To make an impact for God, you must be willing and ready for God to use you.

Your knowledge of God will determine how much impact you make for Him. When the disciples impacted their community, the Pharisees wondered and perceived that they had been with Jesus. This also should be the way people perceive you.

These few truths will prepare you for a closer walk with God. When you pursue to know Him:

1. You can walk with Him, and not know all the details about your destiny.

2. When God makes you a promise, the timeline of the fulfillment is completely up to Him. Abraham waited twenty years for Isaac to be born.

3. Sometimes you will get it wrong before you get it right. Abraham, tired of waiting, ended up fathering Ishmael in an attempt to fulfill God's plan. If he would have just waited, Isaac would have been born on God's schedule. Often your greatest mistakes come from lack of patience.

4. You can have faith in one area, but experience fear in another. When Abraham was to meet with King Abimelech, knowing the king fancied his wife, Abraham called Sarah his sister.

5. Training and education are valuable in the service of the Savior, but nothing can replace time spent in His presence. He is the source of whatever spiritual impact you might have on your world.

How much time have you been spending with Jesus?

BOOK 5
REST IN GREEN PASTURES

Know God, Know Love .... No God, No Love

Power to finish well

Lessons from the Life of Samson

Rest in Green Pastures (R-I-G-P)

CHAPTER 16
KNOW GOD, KNOW LOVE... NO GOD, NO LOVE

...True love is both vertical and horizontal...

John 3:16 – For God so loved the world that He gave His only Son...

It is apparent from this pronouncement that you are loved. No man born of a woman can say you are not loved or nobody loves you. You are an expression of God's love.

Over the eons, others have been at your spot, where they feel unloved and unwanted. Naomi thought she had lost everything, but she had Ruth. Elijah was so lonely he became suicidal. But he had a servant who stuck with him even when he went to the mountainside to hear the voice of God.

God is the author and finisher of love. Read 1 John 4 and discover the depth of God's love to us, which He expects us to transfer.

True love is both vertical and horizontal. Vertical toward God, and horizontal toward men. It is an acceptance and appreciation of the vertical love of God that makes the horizontal relationship with people possible. The greatest commandment in the Bible is centered on relationship (Matthew 22:35-40.)

Vertical relationship (Matthew 22:37.) "You shall love the Lord your God with all of your heart, with all of your soul, and with all of your mind, and with all of your strength."

Horizontal relationship (Matthew 22:39.) "You shall love your neighbor as yourself."

People are the most important assets we have on earth. A good relationship with the people God plants in our lives may determine how far we go in the journey of life. We all need people, in both tangible and intangible ways to move us toward our divine destination in life. To sustain Godly relationship, you need to understand the following:

1. The Law of Respect – defined as the act of placing value on people no matter their status or position but just because they are human beings, loved by God.

2. The Law of Recognition and Encouragement – the challenges of life have hit some people so hard and so repeatedly they have totally lost confidence in themselves. Even if there is a light at the end of the tunnel, they assume the light is a train, not an exit to their darkness. We all need encouragement. We all look forward to being encouraged. We all love encouragement. Try and encourage at least one person every day.

3. The Law of Trust – Joseph had an official business relationship with the head of the prison but he trusted and confided in the butler and the baker. We only share our thoughts with people we trust. Every true relationship is based and sustained on trust! Who do you trust?

Let us use love not only as a seasonal feeling but a life practice. Let it be an outflow of the love you have received from God to all the people you come in contact with, so God may be glorified.

CHAPTER 17
POWER TO FINISH WELL

…enduring faith is more than getting through another year…

It is one thing to start something, and another thing to finish it.

If you look back, I'm sure you can find more than a few projects you left uncompleted. There may still be the exercise machine in the basement. There may still be a book on your shelf you didn't finish reading. There may still be a class you never finished taking. You may have given your life to Christ, but fallen back into your sinful nature.

Imagine spending your lifetime waiting on a promise. Remaining faithful to the promise of the Deliverer means you will have to stick with it, through disappointments and challenges. Your marathon faith would have witnessed many on the side of the road who used to run alongside you, but have given up along the way. Maybe they did not think the journey would be this tough, but when they discovered it was, they stopped the race and left you running alone.

The runner who bolts out of the starting block is full of the expectation of a prize. But enduring faith is more than getting through another year or rushing to finish the long race ahead. Enduring faith believes in the purpose for the race from the beginning, and uses it as strength to continue to the end.

Common sense is not faith, and faith is not common sense. They are as different as the natural life and the spiritual. Simeon and Anna trusted God when common sense ran out. Do you have what it takes to hold on to the promises of God in complete rebellion against your common sense? Can you venture out with courage on the words of Jesus Christ, while the realities of your common sense life continue to shout, "It's all a lie" or "It's not possible?"

When you are going through a mountaintop experience it is easy to believe God and all He says. Eventually you have to travel back down from the mountaintop to the valley, where unbelievers, demons, and life in general ask you questions and mock your "Mount of Transfiguration" belief.

Joseph was hated and betrayed by his own brothers. He was sold into slavery. He became a servant of Potiphar, where he did become the head servant. He was then accused falsely and sent to prison. He lost everything he had gained over the previous years in one instant. He was forgotten by his friends in prison after he had helped them. At the age of 29, he was still a prisoner with no hope in sight ... and age fast caught up with him. Until God's appointed time for his deliverance.

Faith must be tested in order to be strengthened (1 Peter 1:6-8.) If it is never tested, then your faith remains weak. It can only become your most intimate and personal possession through struggle. Sprint races have their place in some situations, but God needs marathon men for His army.

CHAPTER 18
LESSONS FROM THE LIFE OF SAMSON

...Spiritual descent is usually gradual and never instant...

We probably have heard and read a lot about the tragedy of the life of Samson.

However, the truth cannot be over-flogged and lessons over-learnt.

Judges 13:3-5 introduces the prophetic word that would lead and guard the existence of Samson. By all means, many believers would have wished to have a prophetic word so accurate about their lives or that of their children.

For many believers, Samson did not have any excuse to fail. This is why I have extracted two major lessons to be learnt from the life of Samson so we do not fall in the same mistakes.

1. When a leader tends to disregard boundaries and restrictions. The gateway to life is small and the road is narrow (Matthew 7:14.) The Nazirite vow was a destiny boundary for Samson. He was to stay away from things that were unwise, unclean, and unnecessary. This was God's way of keeping him from spinning out of control.

Boundaries are designed to keep us on track and out of trouble. The same traits and gifts that build can lead to destruction if not kept within certain boundaries. Samson was a strong alpha male, daring and impulsive, reckless and carefree. These were traits and qualities that will serve him well as the military commander, but they were also the qualities that got him in trouble.

Spiritual descent is usually gradual and never instant. Samson did not wake up one day to trash his Nazirite vow. He slipped gradually into a life of disobedience by making a series of small compromises.

2. When a leader tends to ignore good advice (Proverbs 12:15.) Samson ultimately married a girl against his parents' wishes and set in motion a chain of events that brought him nothing but frustration and heartache. If you are a leader, you need to ask yourself how you measure up in this area.

- Do you feel embarrassed when you have to ask for advice?

- Do you bristle when someone challenges your way of doing things?

- Have there been times when you have recklessly disregarded good advice just to prove that nobody can tell you what to do?

- Would you admit that you've done some pretty dumb things purely out of stubbornness?

The solution to these is:

- Accept that great men covet good advice. Sometimes we get so engrossed in what we are doing that we don't know what we are doing wrong. Next time someone gives you a piece of advice, be careful how you respond because the person may be looking at something you can't see. The greatest men choose good advisors.

- Listen to people who disagree with you. If you only listen to people who agree with you, your mind will never be stretched, your actions will never be challenged and your course will never be altered, even when it needs to be. The world is full of people who have achieved great success without doing things your way.

- Listen to people who have achieved the success you are looking for.

- Listen to people who demonstrate wisdom (Proverbs 15:7.)

- Listen to people who know and love God's word. When you find a person who knows and loves God's word, someone who has not only studied it but also built their life on its principles and precepts, you need to listen carefully.

- Listen to people who love you. People who love you always have your best interest at heart. These are people who have proven their love over time.

In summary, Samson fell for the old adage that says: if a tree falls in the forest and no one is around to hear it, does it make a sound? In the same way Samson thought that if a man breaks a rule and no one is there to see it, did he actually break the rule? It is a false belief that ultimately led him to his downfall.

CHAPTER 19
REST IN GREEN PASTURES (R-I-G-P)

…Do you truly believe who He says you are in Him?…

The grass seems to always be greener in my neighbor's yard; a statement that indicates several things about someone else.

For instance, the person is somehow living much better than you; the person takes care of their lives better than you take care of your own; things just seem to be working out better for that person than for you.

We all have fallen prey to such a feeling or thought at some point in life. The question I ask though is who is the one tending your life?

Psalms 23 starts off by answering this very question.

"The Lord is my Shepherd, I shall not want" is a statement of release. A shepherd takes care of the needs of the sheep. The sheep only needs to remain in the presence of the shepherd. If the Lord is my Shepherd, I then am His sheep. By such a relation, I only need to remain in the presence of my Shepherd, and He will take care of me. All I need He will provide.

We are constantly busy with the things of life; trying to

succeed, provide food for our families, pay school tuition, etc. We are on our feet, in our cars, in the air, for the most of our lives. The idea to lay down makes one look irresponsible... lazy.

"Your peers are working hard and you are lying down, resting," can be heard ringing in your ears. But that is what is being said in Psalms 23. "He makes you to lie down in green pastures." The very statement of REST. And the truth is written in the fact that when you remain in His presence, when you leave your life in His hand and allow him to take care of your needs, you find there is nothing to do but rest... and no one rests standing up! You are able to lie down in the green pasture, which is your life because your Shepherd is taking care of your needs.

Allow the Lord to make your life a green pasture you can lie in. When you do, there is nothing you will want. I challenge you to seek to remain in His presence, where you will always find His green pastures.

Let's take a closer look at Psalms 23.

R-I-G-P is about the Principle of Trust.

* Do you trust that you are under His grace and no longer under the law of sin & death? Romans 8:2 says, "the law of the spirit of life has made me free from the law of sin & death…"

* Do you truly believe who He says you are in Him? 2 Corinthians 5:17 says, "…new creature in Christ … old things have passed away…"

* Do you believe when He says by His stripes you are healed? Isaiah 53:5.

* Do you believe He took your place on the cross so you could

take His place as a victor? Isaiah 53:4 -6 says, "Our iniquity was laid on him…" and Galatians 3:13 says, "having become a curse for us…"

* Do you believe that He's gone to prepare a place for us? John 14:2-3.

* Do you believe all things are possible to those who believe? Mark 9:23.

Can you swim or float on water? I can swim, but I cannot float. A principle summarizes everything. What does it take to float on water? To float, you need to relax and let go. Now that is strange. How do you let go on top of water? But this principle is the most important about trust. The day you learn to float is the day you enter into His rest.

The reason why Psalms 23 says, "He makes me lie down…" is because it is natural to worry, especially when there are obvious challenges. When your child is in crisis and someone tells you to relax, you will speak a different language. But in the midst of a storm, God makes you and me to lie down. He teaches us to rest in His grace, to rest in His ability, in His strength. That is why He makes us to lie down.

The day you understand what it means and what it takes to float is the day you understand what it means to rest in His green Pastures. In His arms, you are safe. He can handle everything, because He is your shepherd. The duty of the Shepherd is to lead. A sheep does not doubt the ability of the Shepherd; the sheep just follows the Shepherd's lead.

When the Shepherd of your soul leads, you shall not lack. You shall not want, because He is your Shepherd. He leads you besides the still waters. He leads you to drink from peaceful waters. He leads you to the place of green pastures.

When you trust God, your attitude is that of a swimmer, when he/she floats. You can only float on water when you trust and relax (100% trust you will not sink.)

It is time for you to just FLOAT on His word, and then you can truly R-I-G-P!

R-I-G-P is about commitment.

* Psalm 23 speaks about:

"The Lord."

"My shepherd."

"He leads me."

* Commitment to serve in His pastures. Adam was located in the garden to serve - Genesis 1:27-28, 2:8-15.

* Commitment to birth something new. Solomon built the temple when the Lord had granted him peace.

* Commitment to desire His word & spend time studying His word along with good Christian books. I Peter 2:2, John 6:35.

R-I-G-P is about the Kingdom of Christ.

* A kingdom is the domain of a king. Before you can ask for His Kingdom to come into your life, you have to ask your kingdom to go. Rev 11:15 says, "…the kingdom of this world has become the kingdom of our Lord…" and in 2 Corinthians 5:20, "… we are Christ's ambassadors…"

* Before He can be your shepherd, He must be your Lord. The centurion, in Matthew 8:5-13 understood the place of the master perfectly.

* When He is your shepherd, the responsibility of leadership is His while the responsibility of submission is yours. The shepherd only leads His sheep and not goats or sheep belonging to others. The shepherd leads to still waters.

Everyone must access the sheepfold through the Door. John 10:7 says, "…I am the door of the sheepfold…"

GREEN PASTURES CONFESSION

Before He can be your shepherd, you need to make this confession of faith, to trust Him, to be committed to Him, and to confess Him as the Lord over your life and affairs.

I want you to join me in making this confession:

I (insert your name), ——————————————————————,
by the grace of God will depend on the Lord as my Lord and Shepherd for guidance and leadership. The Lord is my shepherd, my shield, and my source. The Lord has anointed my head with oil and I will never lack ointment. I shall not suffer loss or lack.

Through The Lord:

I shall do mighty things.

I shall have rest from sin.

I shall have rest from strife.

I shall have rest in my body.

I shall have rest in my finances.

I shall have rest to worship the Lord.

I shall enjoy the overflow of goodness and mercy.

I shall have rest for creativity that will impact my generation.

We seal this confession with Amen.

CONCLUSION

...you have what it takes to be a success...

The season to succeed is now!

Romans 13:11 (NKJV) says "...knowing the time that now it is high time to awake out of sleep..."

Martin Luther King (1967) had this to say:

"We are now faced with the fact, my friends, that tomorrow is today. We are confronted with the fierce urgency of now. In this unfolding conundrum of life and history, there is such a thing as being too late. Procrastination is still the thief of time. Life often leaves us standing bare, naked, and dejected with a lost opportunity..."

Failure is not an option. Your attitude determines your altitude. The key to your success is in you. This is the time to change the direction of your search for success—inwards.

You have what it takes to be a success.

God bless you, and till we meet to part no more, keep flourishing across the green pastures of His word.

BIBLIOGRAPHY

1. http://www.forbes.com/2010/03/09/worlds-richest-people-slim-gates-buffett-billionaires-2010-intro_slide_2.html

2. http://www.notable-quotes.com/f/franklin_benjamin.html

3. http://www.bereanwife.net/tag/a-w-tozer/

4. The 7 Habits of Highly Effective People by Stephen Covey, Free Press, 1989

5. http://en.wikipedia.org/wiki/Ken_Griffey,_Jr.

6. http://www.lesbrown.com/

7. http://www.gbcdecatur.org/sermons/AboutTime.html

8. Dr. Ed Clavell https://sermons.logos.com/submissions/43840-Family-T-I-M-E-#content=/submissions/43840

9. http://www.infidelityfacts.com/infidelity-statistics.html

10. https://www.goodreads.com/quotes/100469-we-are-now-faced-with-the-fact-that-tomorrow-is

11. http://www.sermoncentral.com/sermons/god-can-michael-luke-sermon-on-god-the-father-79836.asp

12. http://en.wikipedia.org/wiki/Jim_Croce

13. https://www.goodreads.com/author/quotes/40328.Billy_Graham

14. http://en.wikipedia.org/wiki/Emmitt_Smith

ABOUT THE AUTHOR

Bayo Fadugba is the Senior Pastor of The Redeemed Christian Church of God, Dominion Chapel, Stafford, Texas. He has been in ministry for about twenty years, consistently preaching a message of faith, salvation and victorious living in Christ. His ministry is characterized by his compassionate and loving heart, and a strong desire to help people fulfill their divine destiny.

A trained attorney by profession, Bayo is married to his college sweetheart Toun, and they live with their three sons in Sugar Land, Texas.

CONNECT

To connect with Pastor Bayo Fadugba today,

Email:

pastorb@dominionchapel.org

Facebook:

www.facebook.com/bayo.fadugba.7

Twitter:

@PstBayo

Visit:

books.Godkulture.org/BayoFadugba